THE Mechanics of School Counseling

WORKBOOK

National Center for Youth Issues
Practical Guidance Resources
Educators Can Trust

ncyi.org

P.O. Box 22185 • Chattanooga, TN 37422-2185
423.899.5714 • 800.477.8277
fax: 423.899.4547 • www.ncyi.org

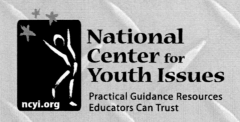

National Center for Youth Issues
Practical Guidance Resources
Educators Can Trust
ncyi.org

P.O. Box 22185
Chattanooga, TN 37422-2185
423.899.5714 • 800.477.8277
fax: 423.899.4547
www.ncyi.org

ISBN: 978-1-937870-33-1
© 2014 National Center for Youth Issues, Chattanooga, TN
All rights reserved.

Written by: Eric Chancy
Contributing Authors: Kerri Bridges and Katy Rabon Elkins
Edited by: Beth Rabon
Cover Design and Page Layout: Phillip Rodgers
Published by National Center for Youth Issues

Printed at Starkey Printing • Chattanooga, TN, USA • December 2014

Table of Contents

THE Mechanics of School Counseling WORKBOOK

getting Started

You're at a new school. Whether you're a veteran of schools just changing schools or you're a brand new counselor, the transition and learning all the names and details can be grueling. This workbook is designed to help you adapt, and while it cannot speak to each and every situation, we have worked hard to cover a great deal of ground. The object is to get you intentionally "in the know" about commonalities among schools and how school counselors work, interact and function in and with those schools, instead of haphazardly pursuing information only when the need arises.

You have a steep learning curve. Take a deep breath, and work through this material, knowing that in the end, you will have collective knowledge from which many people, including students, parents, teachers and colleagues may benefit.

From where can I find a job description of a school counselor:

The school / district? _____

The state? _____

What are my primary roles and functions going to be?

_____

_____

What is my caseload assignment?

_____

_____

What are my departmental responsibilities?

_____

_____

Will I be assigned to any school committees?

_____

_____

Are there any before or after school duties to which I will be assigned?

_____

_____

Will I be given any club or extracurricular responsibilities? _____

Where can I find a copy of the district board policy? _____

Where can I obtain a copy of the Student Handbook, with the Code of Conduct, dress code, etc.? _____

THE Mechanics *of* School Counseling WORKBOOK

the Players

District Personnel

Please obtain the names and other information for the following:

Who is your Superintendent?

Name:_____

Background:_____

_____

Assistant Superintendents

Name any and all. Highlight the one(s) most relevant to your school scenario.

_____   _____

_____   _____

_____   _____

Directors and Supervisors of School Counseling Services

Names and responsibilities. Highlight those most relevant to your school scenario.

_____   _____

_____   _____

_____   _____

Who is your school Principal?

Name:_____

Background:_____

_____

_____

Assistant Principal(s)

Check applicable responsibilities:

☐ Student-related
☐ Staff-related
☐ Building-related

Details:_____

_____

Assistant Principal(s)

Check applicable responsibilities:
- ☐ Student-related
- ☐ Staff-related
- ☐ Building-related

Details:_____

_____

Assistant Principal(s)

Check applicable responsibilities:
- ☐ Student-related
- ☐ Staff-related
- ☐ Building-related

Details:_____

_____

Principal's Secretary

Name:_____

Background:_____

_____

Main office personnel and primary functions:

_____   _____

_____   _____

_____   _____

Please locate the following items, if **applicable**:

- School District Mission Statement
- School District Philosophy and Vision
- School Mission Statement

- School Philosophy and Vision
- Student Services/Guidance Mission Statement
- Student Services/Guidance Philosophy and Vision

Guidance/Student Services Personnel

Please obtain the names and other information for the following people:

Receptionist: _____

Lead Counselor/Department Chair

Name: _____

Caseload: _____

Primary functions: _____

Secondary functions: _____

Counselor

Name: _____

Caseload: _____

Primary functions: _____

Secondary functions: _____

Counselor

Name: _____

Caseload: _____

Primary functions: _____

Secondary functions: _____

Counselor

Name: _____

Caseload: _____

Primary functions: _____

Secondary functions: _____

Counselor

Name: _____

Caseload: _____

Primary functions: _____

Secondary functions: _____

Data / Student Information Systems Manager

Name:_____

Email and phone: _____

Who else handles information technology issues in our building? (Include location/contact info)

_____

_____

Does the school have a test coordinator?   ☐ Yes ☐ No

If so, whom?_____

Is there a testing calendar I can access?   ☐ Yes ☐ No

Where can it be found? (Attach a copy if possible) _____

_____

What are the standardized tests that will affect our students? _____

_____

Are translation services available in the building? ☐ Yes ☐ No

If so, by whom? _____

Does our department hold any standing meetings? ☐ Yes ☐ No

Day_____   Time_____

School address _____

Department fax_____

How do I gain entry for events after normal hours? _____

From whom should I obtain business cards? _____

Is there a staff handbook? (May I have one?) _____

Media Center Staff

Please locate your Media Center/Library and become familiar with the staff.

Staff member: _____

Position: _____

Responsibilities: _____

_____

Staff member: _____

Position: _____

Responsibilities: _____

_____

Staff member: _____

Position: _____

Responsibilities: _____

Custodial Staff

How do I contact custodial staff should the need arise?

_____

Head Custodian: _____

Hours on campus: _____

Custodian: _____ Hours on campus: _____

Custodian: _____ Hours on campus: _____

Custodian: _____ Hours on campus: _____

Custodian: _____ Hours on campus: _____

Custodian: _____ Hours on campus: _____

Custodian: _____ Hours on campus: _____

Custodian: _____ Hours on campus: _____

Custodian: _____ Hours on campus: _____

working with
Educators

Our core business as a school is education. The bulk of the work within that core business is being performed by and engaged in by teachers and students. To some degree, that already creates an "Us / Them" relationship. If your message to teachers is that your business is more important than theirs, it becomes nearly impossible to work in unison toward the common goal of educating children. Mutual respect is vital in our work, so please communicate to your teachers that you will make every effort to respect their time with their students, and that there are occasions where calling a student from that class cannot be avoided.

Discovering the interests and passions of individuals connects you on a personal level. Everyone is more than just the position they hold. Here, you will list the school personnel, and something that they are passionate about. This is not an "opening day" exercise, but is about building rapport and credibility over time instead. You will have to talk with them–sometimes one on one and sometimes in groups. In either case, remember to come back and jot down that Mr. Greer is passionate about knitting, or that Mrs. Lasher's interests outside of school involve dogs, particularly Huskies.

Teacher	Passionate Interest

Teacher	Passionate Interest

Teacher   **Passionate Interest**

Teacher	Passionate Interest

Teacher	Passionate Interest

Teacher   **Passionate Interest**

Teacher	Passionate Interest

Curriculum

Where can I locate the specifics on the curriculum required in this state?

Website: _____

If different, Where can I locate the specifics on the curriculum required in this district?

Website: _____

Is there curriculum that is only available or is specifically lacking in my district? (I.E., We have the only Medical Science program in the state, or alternatively, we are the only district in the state that does not have any computer programming coursework.)

☐ Yes ☐ No   Explain: _____

_____

Is there curriculum that is only available or is specifically lacking in this school?

☐ Yes ☐ No   Explain: _____

_____

Are there opportunities in the school for students to enhance their interest in curriculum (magnet programming, academically gifted programming, etc.)?

☐ Yes ☐ No

If so, how do students and parents access information about those opportunities? _____

_____

_____

Is there a specific person who focuses on academically gifted / talented students?

☐ Yes ☐ No   Name: _____

Who evaluates transfer records for grade level and curriculum placement?

_____

What standardized documentation will be used to help evaluate those records?

(Are there specific forms we use?) _____

_____

Special Education

Who is the special education lead for your school?

_____

PLEASE OBTAIN THE FOLLOWING INFORMATION FROM YOUR SPECIAL EDUCATION LEAD

Who are the case managers for your school?

_____   _____

_____   _____

_____   _____

_____   _____

_____   _____

When working with parents and students, how do I know which case manager serves a student?

_____

Who is expected to attend IEP meetings? (Which staff members?)

_____   _____

_____   _____

_____   _____

Will I be notified of meetings for my students? ☐ Yes ☐ No

If so, by whom: _____

How? _____

What role will I be asked to play in IEP meetings, if any? _____

_____

Will I be apprised of changes to the IEP? ☐ Yes ☐ No

If so, by whom: _____

How? _____

Who functionally makes any classroom or coursework changes originated through special education?

Name:_____

How does the Special Education referral process work in this state?

_____
_____
_____

In this district?

_____
_____
_____

In this school? (For this section, you want to outline the process, including names.)

_____
_____
_____
_____
_____
_____

504 Plan

How does a 504 plan differ from the processes outlined above?_____

_____
_____
_____

Who is in charge of the 504 plan for a student?

Name: _____

When documentation is provided by outside agencies regarding the diagnosis of a disability, to whom does it go?

Name:_____

What are my responsibilities for following up on the special education process?_____

_____

_____

_____

How does the RTI (Repsonse to Intervention) process work in this state? _____

_____

_____

_____

In this district? _____

_____

_____

_____

In this school? (For this section, you want to outline the process, including names.)

_____

_____

_____

_____

_____

_____

_____

THE
Mechanics
of
School
Counseling
WORKBOOK

working with
Social Workers,
School Health Services
& School Psychologists

Social Workers

Who are the social workers I will work with in this building?

Person:_____

On-campus days/hours:_____

_____

Role:_____

_____

Person:_____

On-campus days/hours:_____

_____

Role:_____

_____

Person:_____

On-campus days/hours:_____

_____

Role:_____

_____

Who oversees the social workers employed by our district?

Names and responsibilities. Highlight those most relevant to your school scenario.

_____   _____

_____   _____

_____   _____

_____   _____

_____   _____

Which county or other agency handles social work outside of our system, but in our community?

Agency Name: _____

Phone: _____ Website: _____

Reporting to state agencies

What information am I allowed to provide and to whom?

_____

_____

What documentation am I required to collect?

_____

_____

What is the protocol and requirement in this state for reporting suspected abuse?

_____

_____

What is the protocol in this district for reporting suspected abuse?

_____

_____

What is the protocol in this building for reporting suspected abuse?

_____

_____

School Health Services

Some schools have a nurse on staff daily, and others only benefit from that person's help once a week.

Name: _____

Days at school each week: _____

_____

How are students referred to the nurse? _____

_____

What are the limits and boundaries of your school nurse's scope of work? _____

_____

_____

_____

_____

What are you permitted to do, and what are you not permitted to do?_____

_____

_____

_____

_____

School Psychologists

Name:_____

Email: _____

Phone: _____

Functions: _____

_____

_____

_____

_____

_____

_____

Procedures for
Getting the
Job Done

Bus Duty

What are the expectations of me during morning and afternoon drop off?

_____

_____

_____

Career Development

Who is the point of contact for career development at your school?

Name: _____

Please check one:

☐ This person is a **dedicated staff member** who heads up career development.

☐ This is an **additional function** of a counseling staff member.

Annual Career Development Activities conducted (please list):

_____

_____

Monthly Career Development Activities conducted:

_____

_____

Opportunities for me to be involved in classroom career development:

_____

_____

Opportunities for me to be involved in school-wide career development:

_____

_____

Lunch Duty

What are the expectations of me during lunch?

_____

_____

Class / Group Presentations

How and where do we present information to large groups? _____

_____

Do we need to bring additional equipment in order to provide information in these locations?

☐ Yes ☐ No

If yes, what equipment? _____

_____

Where does the equipment come from?: _____

_____

Have a departmental conversation (not recorded here) about which teachers have historically been most amenable to counselor presentations.

Handling Parent and Student Concerns

Are the district expectations for handling concerns spelled out anywhere?

☐ Yes ☐ No   Location: _____

Is there a directive as to how to handle a concern that goes beyond the counseling office?

Check any / all as appropriate:

☐ Student or parent should meet with and address directly with teacher, if not done already;

☐ Counselor hears out concern, obtains information from teacher, reports back to parent/ student, determines course of action and plan

☐ Counselor hears out concern and refers to administrator

☐ Other: _____

Respecting Class Time

When is it considered reasonable of me to call for a student?

☐ During electives

☐ Only during lunch time

☐ Any time is fine

Resolving Conflicts with Teachers

Even the best of professionals disagree. Not everyone always bears the same professional opinion, and your opinion that you need to see a student to resolve an issue may meet with resistance against Mrs. Lawrence's opinion that the student is better served preparing for the upcoming choral concert.

When you have a concern about the practices of a teacher, whether related to school counseling or related to their classroom and students, you need to know the expectations of the administration. Keep in mind that if a teacher has concerns about you, you would prefer to have the first opportunity to resolve the conflict. Counselors should always work to model positive behaviors and resolution for students and colleagues. Counselors and teachers are not on different tiers. They have different roles, but are working at the same level and with the same goal – the best education for the student.

When I have concerns about a teacher, do I:
(Check one or more as appropriate, and number in order of departmental protocol)

☐ ___ address the concern directly with the teacher;

☐ ___ consult with my colleagues to see if their experience is the same;

☐ ___ discuss with the lead counselor/department supervisor;

☐ ___ Other: _____

Student Transportation

This will not be a huge issue in most districts, but in some high-population districts, how to navigate transportation could be consuming.

Where can I access information on student transportation, including bus lists?

_____

_____

What information is readily and publicly accessible?

_____

_____

Is there a process for requesting alternate transportation, and to whom does it apply (Special Education, magnet or academically gifted situations, etc.)?

_____

_____

Technology

What types of technology will need to be utilized within the context of performing the daily work in this department?

_____

_____

What software / student information databases will I need to become familiar with to use on a regular basis in this department?

_____

_____

_____

Is there additional technology / technology support throughout the _building?_ (Hardware, licensed software, in-house tech training, etc.) If so, list below.

_____

_____

_____

Is there additional technology / technology support throughout the _district?_ (Hardware, licensed software, in-house tech training, etc.) If so, list below.

_____

_____

_____

Who is responsible for the Student Services/Guidance website? (Please review website with supervisor)

_____

Who manages our school's social media?

_____

Who manages our Student Services/Guidance social media?

_____

Resources for
Moving Ahead

Jot things down in this section that you hear about, want to investigate or know can be of benefit to your students/community!

_____
_____
_____
_____
_____
_____
_____
_____
_____
_____
_____
_____
_____
_____
_____
_____
_____
_____
_____
_____
_____
_____
_____
_____
_____
_____

Is there a formal process for scheduling in-class guidance session for our students with our teachers?

☐ Yes ☐ No

If yes, what is that process? _____

_____

_____

Pre-Kindergarten Services

What office handles the Pre-Kindergarten services in our district?

_____

Elementary School

Where can I obtain the state curriculum for K-5 counseling?

_____

_____

_____

How has this curriculum been implemented previously at this school?

_____

_____

_____

What is the process for identifying elementary students for *Special Education*?

_____

_____

_____

_____

What is the process for identifying elementary students for *Academically Gifted and Talented*?

_____

_____

_____

_____

How are our students organized, (teams, groups, etc) and how is that decided?

_____

_____

How are students chosen for accelerated classes?

_____

_____

Registration for the Next Year
(Grade 8 leaving to high school)

When does it start? (Month): _____

When does it end? (Month): _____

How do we communicate registration information to students?

_____

_____

How do we communicate registration information to parents?

_____

_____

How do we communicate registration information to staff?

_____

_____

How are registration changes requested?

_____

_____

What is the process for current year coursework changes?

_____

_____

High School

Is there a standard process for recording progress toward graduation?

_____

_____

Scholarships and Financial Aid

Who is the financial aid wizard at our school?

Name: _____

How in depth am I expected to know financial aid before I refer to the financial aid liaison?

Please check those applicable:

☐ Refer immediately

☐ Review FAFSA timeline, postsecondary institution financial aid requirements, scholarship opportunities

☐ I am responsible for walking my students through the entire financial aid process

☐ Other: _____

Transcripts

What information is included on our transcript?

_____

_____

What information is excluded?

_____

_____

How are they requested?

_____

_____

Is there a fee? ☐ Yes ☐ No

To whom does that request go?

Name: _____

How it is processed?

Please check those applicable:

☐ Electronically/digitally

☐ manually/hard copy

☐ both

How can parents / students check on the status of a transcript request?

_____

_____

Registration for Next School Year

When does it start? (Month): _____

When does it end? (Month): _____

How do we communicate registration information to students?

_____

_____

How do we communicate registration information to parents?

_____

_____

How do we communicate registration information to staff?

_____

_____

How are registration changes requested?

_____

_____

Do students develop a four-year curriculum plan to assist with year-to-year registration?

☐ Yes ☐ No

Who is responsible for record-keeping related to registration (special course requests, external courses at other schools, online coursework, etc)?

Name: _____

What is the process for current year coursework changes?

_____

_____

_____